The
Nature
Puzzle Book

Scholastic Publications Ltd,
10 Earlham Street, London WC2H 9RX, UK

Scholastic Inc,
730 Broadway, New York, NY 10003, USA

Scholastic Tab Publications Ltd,
123 Newkirk Road, Richmond Hill,
Ontario L4C 3G5, Canada

Ashton Scholastic Pty Ltd,
P O Box 579, Gosford, New South Wales,
Australia

Ashton Scholastic Ltd,
165 Marua Road, Panmure, Auckland 6,
New Zealand

First published by
Scholastic Publications Ltd, 1990

ISBN 0 590 76199 4

Made and printed by Cox and Wyman Ltd.,
Reading, Berks.

Typeset in Helvetica by COLLAGE (Design in Print)
Longfield Hill, Kent.

10 9 8 7 6 5 4 3 2 1

The
Nature
Puzzle Book

Ron Wilson

Illustrated by Mike Dodd

Danny

Hippo Books
Scholastic Publications Limited
London

**To Sarah
who helped out
when things were difficult.**

ANIMALS AND PLANTS

Take an animal from the left-hand list and add it to
a word from the right-hand list to make the name
of a plant or animal.

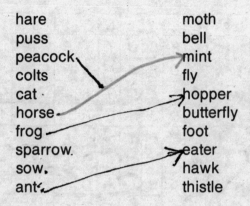

hare	moth
puss	bell
peacock	mint
colts	fly
cat	hopper
horse	butterfly
frog	foot
sparrow	eater
sow	hawk
ant	thistle

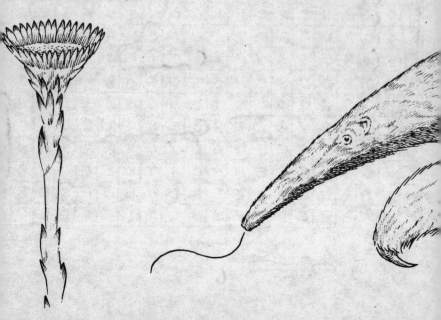

FIND THE 'MINIBEASTS'

Hidden in the square are the names of a number of 'minibeasts'. They are all listed on page 7. See how many you can find.

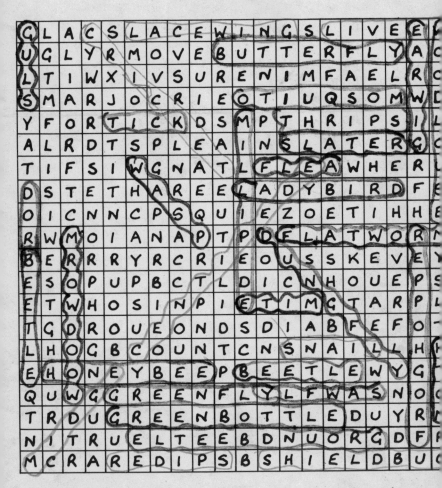

honeybee	aphid	lacewing ✓	wasp ✓
beetle ✓	ant ✓	weevil ✓	tick ✓
greenfly ✓	mite ✓	butterfly ✓	froghopper ✓
greenbottle ✓	gnat	cricket ✓	moth ✓
spider ✓	thrips ✓	flea ✓	groundbeetle ✓
shieldbug	slater ✓	ladybird ✓	mosquito ✓
midge ✓	woodworm	woodlouse ✓	millipede ✓
centipede ✓	leafminer ✓	flatworm ✓	sawfly ✓
scorpion	dungfly ✓	hoverfly	earwig ✓
cranefly	slug ✓	snail ✓	dorbeetle ✓

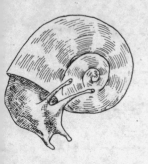

BERRIES

When you have solved the clues below, add the word 'berry' to find the answer.

1 A person who isn't young.

_ _ _ _ _ berry

2 A measure of herrings. _ _ _ _ berry

3 It comes in winter. _ _ _ _ berry

4 The opposite of white. _ _ _ _ _ berry

5 This is left after cutting the corn.

_ _ _ _ _ berry

6 A boy's name — short for William.

_ _ _ berry

7 A web-footed bird. _ _ _ _ _ berry

8 To make a scraping noise. _ _ _ _ berry

9 _ _ _ _ of Kintyre. _ _ _ berry

10 The colour of the sky. _ _ _ _ berry

FIND THE YOUNG

The adult names of various animals are given below. Do you know what their young are called?

	Adult	Young
1	leopard	
2	sheep	Lamb
3	dog	puppy
4	horse	fowl
5	goose	gosling
6	hen	chicken
7	pig	piglet
8	swan	signet
9	cow	calf
10	hare	
11	deer	fow
12	cat	Kitten	Kitten

WELL HIDDEN

All sorts of animals are hidden in the sentences below. See how quickly you can spot them. To help you we've completed the first one for you.

1. That's my money, give me half <u>Roger</u> please.

2. I wish you would let me have a go at the new game you bought.

3. I am not very keen on men who have beards.

4. Did your char ever leave you alone?

5. I wish I could make my first million quickly.

6. The vase always looks better with roses in it.

7. For prestige remember that we all went to University.

8. I need some calico when you go to town.

9. I hear that you went to a dinner last Thursday.

10. It's rather unusual to find a house here.

11 John is a sensible person, he abhors every kind of violence.

12 I need all the help I can get with this new venture.

13 Please try to be a very good girl.

14 If you do give to charities, make sure that they are genuine.

15 He only made a little murmur when I called him.

16 You should inform Simon keys are kept in the porter's office.

17 The shot terrified me as I was nearly asleep.

18 Please let me have a new bike as soon as possible.

19 I shouldn't let you catch him playing his new guitar.

20 This slot here is for five pence pieces.

ODDBODLAND BIRDS

In Oddbodland they spell the names of their birds in a strange way. They use the same letters as we do, but in a different order. Can you make these Oddbodland birds into English birds by re-arranging the letters?

1. fferelaid
2. dbbalkric
3. gsntialr
4. eoprsy
5. nboir
6. skdernha
7. troacyehcsret
8. gwderni
9. nntgae
10. ssroablta

ANIMAL SAYINGS

Below are ten well-known sayings which each
have the name of an animal in them. Can you find
an animal to complete each saying?

1 To let the _ _ _ out of the bag.

2 As quiet as a _ _ _ _ _ .

3 To buy a _ _ _ in a poke.

4 To keep the _ _ _ _ from the door.

5 Straight from the _ _ _ _ _ _ mouth.

6 As cunning as a _ _ _ .

7 As gentle as a _ _ _ _ .

8 A _ _ _ _ in _ _ _ _ _ _ clothing.

9 As busy as a _ _ _ .

10 As strong as an _ _ .

PENGUINS

In the drawing of the penguin below are the names of seven types of penguin. We have muddled up the letters. Can you sort them out?

buth mold

porko perch

too neg

al dee

remrope

or lay

gink

MONKEYS AND APES

Jumbled in the monkey below are the names of five other monkeys and apes. See how quickly you can sort them out.

lrgiola
gorilla

bobaon
baboon

tnua-garon

merul

ezchmpenai
chimpanze

AGAINST THE WALL

The answers to all these questions can be added to WALL to make the name of a plant or animal.

1. Tom never remembered his schooldays.

   wall never

2. Ivy is one, it's true — and so is the bird which has tree in its name.

   wall climber

3. Petals and sepals are among its make-up.

   wall _____

4. You use this for seasoning — but too much might make you sneeze.

   wall _____

5. To regret — or a bitter-leaved shrub.

   wall ___

MUDDLED ANIMALS

We've had a few problems with the typewriter. It jumbled up the names of all these animals. Can you sort them out?

1 ffagire

2 ettroios

3 yemnok

4 lsaenoi

5 oduremso

6 ttreo

7 veraeb

8 tenlpeah

9 laorgli

10 adpna

HEADS AND TAILS

The letters given are just the middle part of the name of a bird or animal. All you have to do is to add the two letters at the beginning and the two at the end.

1 _ _ r u _ _

2 _ _ a r r _ _

3 _ _ l l a _ _

4 _ _ n k _ _

5 _ _ n d _ _

6 _ _ o u _ _

7 _ _ g h o _ _

8 _ _ t t e _ _

9 _ _ a l o _ _

10 _ _ p a _ _

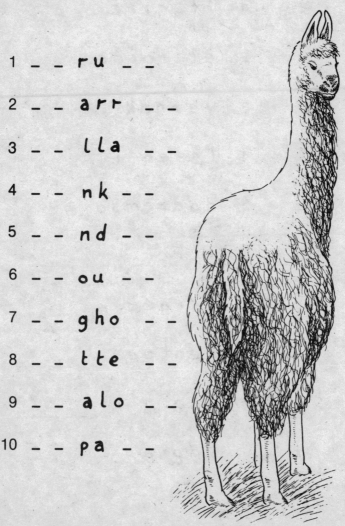

FRUIT SALAD

Solve the clues below and fill in the blanks to find seven fruits. Then the figure in brackets before each clue tells you which letter to take from each answer to find yet another fruit.

Clues

1 Cox's Orange Pippin or Granny Smith's.

(1) _ _ _ _ _

2 Victoria maybe?

(1) _ _ _ _

3 King William is one variety and Conference another.

(4) _ _ _ _

4 Tropical fruit with a small hard shell.

(5) _ _ _ _ _ _ _ _ _ _ _ _

5 Small red or black fruit hanging in clusters.

(1) _ _ _ _ _ _

6 Often used in squash.

(1) _ _ _ _ _ _

7 Usually eaten at breakfast time.

(10) _ _ _ _ _ _ _ _ _ _

New Fruit _ _ _ _ _ _ _

ON THE FARM

The pig is a familiar animal on the farm. So are all the other animals which are jumbled up inside the pig! Rearrange the letters to find out who lives on the farm.

tca

ogesehpd

kyurte

mbla

hpees

llbu

rsohe

nkdyeo

rema

lafo

BOOKS AND FILMS

There are many book and film titles which either have the names of animals in them, or are associated with animals. Some of these titles are jumbled up below. See if you can sort out the words to find the ten titles.

1 Wind in the Otter

2 Ring of Beauty

3 Tarka Book

4 Black the Willows

5 The Living Bright Water

6 Serengeti Desert

7 The Running Shall Not Die

8 The Jungle Foxes

9 Call of the Down

10 Watership Wild

PARTS OF THE BODY

Match a part of the body with each of the words below and you'll end up with the name of a plant or animal!

1   On the end of your leg.

colts _ _ _ _

2   Five of them are attached to each foot.

mistle _ _ _

3   Found on your head.

_ _ _ _ streak butterfly

4   Two are found at the 'entrance' to your mouth.

ox _ _ _

5   Useful for seeing with.

ox _ _ _ daisy

6   You hear with this.

_ _ _ wig

7   Pumps blood round your body.

_ _ _ _ _ sease

8   An organ of the body we call offal when we eat it!

_ _ _ _ _ wort

9 You use this when talking.

adders _ _ _ _ _ _

10 You have a pair of them to walk on.

daddy long _ _ _ _

11 There's one of these on each hand.

millers _ _ _ _ _

12 At the front of the neck.

white _ _ _ _ _ _

13 An organ in the abdomen.

_ _ _ _ _ _ _ wort

14 There are five on your hand.

lady's _ _ _ _ _ _ _

15 It breathes in oxygen from the air.

_ _ _ _ fish

16 Usually eaten with steak.

_ _ _ _ _ _ vetch

17 You find this at the end of a finger or toe.

s _ _ _ _

18 This travels around in your arteries and veins.

_ _ _ _ _ worm

BIRDS IN A MUDDLE

We've had great trouble with our birds and muddled up their names. Can you sort them out?

1 tawny harrier
2 marsh pipit
3 gold shank
4 spotted sparrow
5 tree plover
6 green crake
7 pied grouse
8 red flycatcher
9 sand dove
10 rock gull

11 little sandpiper
12 common bunting
13 hen finch
14 corn warbler
15 wood martin
16 house creeper
17 collared owl
18 reed crest
19 black wagtail
20 grey tern

1. tawny owl
2.

A FRUITY PROBLEM

Fill in the spaces in the apple below to make a
number of fruits across the page. Do this correctly
and you will find the name of another fruit down
the centre!

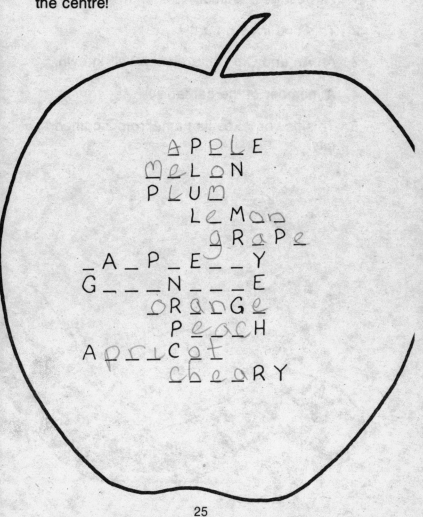

```
    A P P L E
  M E L O N
  P L U M
      L E M O N
        G R A P E
_ A _ P _ E _ _ Y
G _ _ _ N _ _ _ E
      O R A N G E
        P E A C H
A P R I C O T
      C H E R R Y
```

ANTS IN THE ANSWERS

Here is a hint! The word **ant** appears in the answers to all the clues below.

1 Largest land animal.

2 This one lives on ants!

3 An An and Chi Chi are very well-known.

4 A member of the cat family.

5 This flower takes its name from a cathedral city.

CREATURES OF THE WATERS

We may not know whether the Loch Ness Monster really exists, but the strange animals jumbled in this drawing are real enough. Can you match each of the jumbled names with one of the animals in the drawing?

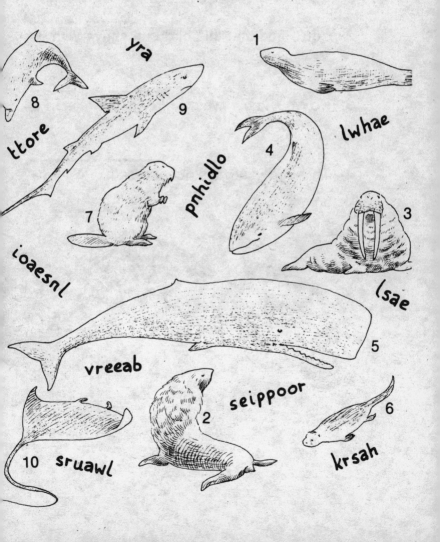

RIDDLED BIRDS

Can you solve these riddles to find the name of a bird each time?

1　This bird begins at the end and has the colour of blood at the beginning.

　　　　　　　　_ _ _ _ _ _ _ _

2　You'll find that this bird can shave with its beak.

　　　　　　　　_ _ _ _ _ - _ _ _ _

3　Do you know which bird is out late in a storm?

　　　　　　　　_ _ _ _ _ _ _ _ _ _

4　This bird is always out of breath.

　　　　　　　　_ _ _ _ _ _

5   Fishermen and scouts might tie one of these.

— — — —

6   You might almost be this if you were attacked by a dog.

— — — — — — —

7   Which bird is a **hard** peacemaker?

— — — — — — — —

8   If you want to change direction and go back, you will have to do this.

— — — —

9   If you're in a hurry you'll have to move like this bird.

— — — — —

10 This has a different spelling when it's part of a flower.

29

— — — — —

WILDLIFE IN DANGER

1 This rare British bird can turn its neck right round to see what is going on behind it. This is how it gets its name. Which bird is it?

2 This small British mammal, known as the 'dozey mouse', is a protected species. What is its proper name?

3 Which is the world's largest living mammal?

4 Which bird, found in reedbeds, is known from the booming cry of the male?

5 The female bird is known as the reeve. What is the name for the male?

6 Which rare owl returned to breed on Fetlar in the Shetlands?

7 Where does the rare bird known as the Takahe live?

8 Britain has one wild cat. What is it called?

9 Fly and Man are types of which rare plant?

10 This mammal, which lives in Tasmania, is known as the Thylacine — and is thought to be extinct now. What is its other name?

11 The white rhino is rare. But white isn't the colour of its skin. What does the word white mean?

12 Which elephant is now close to extinction because people hunt it for its tusks?

13 This gazelle is now found only in the Kalahari Desert and springs lightly into the air when disturbed, hence part of its name. What is it called?

14 The ne ne was bred at the Wildfowl Trust's Slimbridge Reserve and some were returned to their native Japan. What sort of animal is it?

15 The nightingale is quite rare in Britain where it comes to breed. At what time of day does it sing?

16 This rare warbler is named after a town in Kent. Which one?

17 This butterfly became extinct but has been reintroduced to Britain. It needs ants at a certain point in its life cycle. Which butterfly is it?

18 There are three snakes in Britain, one of which is rare. Which is the rare one? What are the other two snakes called?

19 One owl, which used to live in farm buildings, is now in danger. Which owl is it?

20 Which bird of prey, once common in London, now is one of the rarest breeding birds in Wales, where it nests?

THE NAME GAME

There are many plants with boys and girls names in them. We put this list together rather hastily, so unfortunately the names are rather muddled. To find the correct names you will need to pair a word in the first column with a word in the second. Each answer must have a boy's or a girl's name in it.

1	Sweet	Wort
2	Jack	Of-the-Valley
3	Pearl	Violet
4	Herb	Myrtle
5	Lily	Fir
6	Jacob's	Ivy
7	Wild	Bob
8	Douglas	By-the-hedge
9	Creeping	William
10	Bog	Robert
11	Ground	Ladder
12	Dog	Daisy
13	Ox-eye	Pansy
14	Stinking	Jenny
15	Field	Rose

ADD A WORD

Find a one word answer to each of these clues.
Put the words together with the letters given and
you'll end up with the name of a plant or animal.

1 Add a strong animal to get a cunning one.

f _ _

2 Usually used with a pen.

m _ _ _

3 A game or a label.

s _ _ _

4 Another word for pinch, when you do it to
someone.

s _ _ _ e

5 Wheat, oats and rye are all types of this.

a _ _ _ _

6 Part of a flower.

p _ _ _ _ _ _

7 You might have a cup of this at breakfast.

_ _ _ l

8 A cereal crop that's used for porridge.

g _ _ _

9 You might wear one of these to show you
belong to a certain club.

_ _ _ _ _ r

IN THE BIBLE

Many animals are mentioned in the Bible. We've put some of them in Noah's Ark, but muddled up the letters. Sort them out to discover which animals Noah took with him.

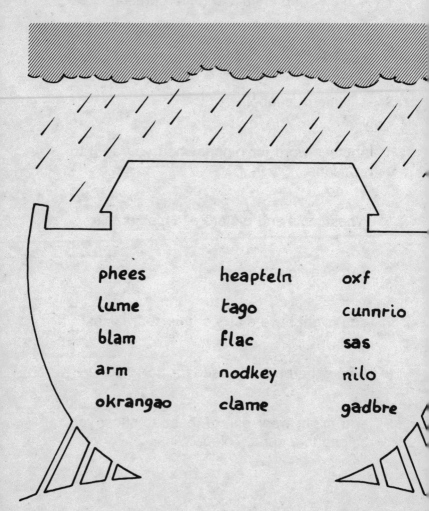

phees

lume

blam

arm

okrangao

heapteln

tago

flac

nodkey

clame

oxf

cunnrio

sas

nilo

gadbre

BIRD RIDDLE

Work out the clue in each line of this riddle and
you should find the letters that make up the name
of a well-known bird.

My first is in Swallow and also in Swift.

My second in pink but not in thrift.

My third in Harp and also in Seal.

My fourth in Mallard but never in Teal.

My fifth in Robin and also in breast.

My sixth in gold but not in crest.

My last in Wren but not in Jenny.

My whole is a bird of which there are many.

ANIMAL OUTLINES

Can you work out the names of these animals just by looking at their outlines?

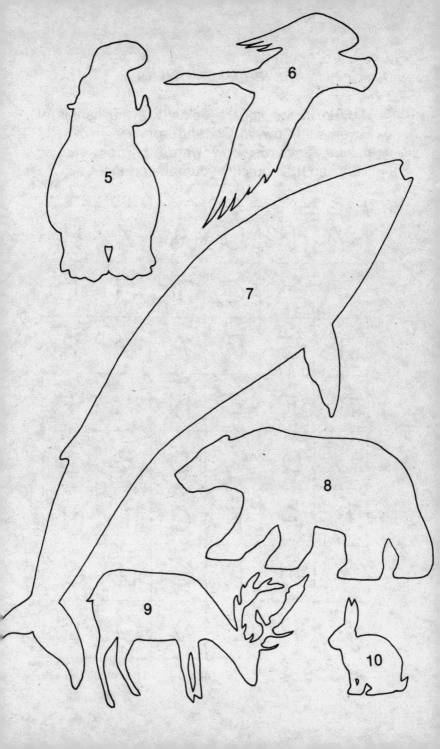

HIDDEN FLOWERS

Hidden in the square below are the names of seven wild flowers. Starting from the arrow and moving upwards, downwards, or from side to side, see how quickly you can find them all.

Y	P	U	A	E	H
V	I	C	T	H	E
T	E	R	A	D	R
T	E	E	N	L	I
U	D	W	D	E	O
B	P	K	C	I	N
Y	O	R	C	H	C
P	P	E	V	O	L

CRAFTY CREATURES

All the animals which fit into the squares below begin with the letter **C**. Clues have been given to help you.

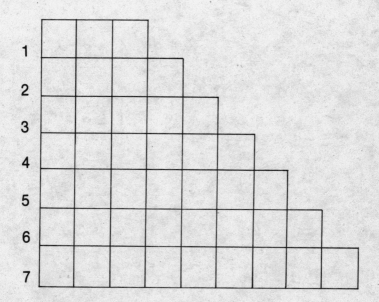

Clues

1 Tabby or tortoiseshell?
2 Another name for guinea pig.
3 Could have one hump or two.
4 Prairie wolf of North America.
5 Definitely the fastest land mammal.
6 A striped ground squirrel.
7 A thick-skinned reptile that lives in water.

SPACES FOR BIRDS

Can you fill in the blanks in the list below to find the names of 20 birds?

1 h _ r _ i _ g _ u _ l

2 _ l _ c _ b _ r _

3 s _ a _ l _ n _

4 _ i _ g _ i _ h _ r

5 _ l _ a _ r _ s _

6 s _ e _ r _ a _ e _

7 c _ a _ f _ n _ h

8 c _ r _ o _ a _ t

9 _ a _ t _ i _ g _

10 d _ b _ h _ c _

11 _ u _ l _ e _ o _

12 f _ y _ a _ c _ e _

13 _ i _ t _ w _ k _

14 l _ p _ i _ g

15 _ i _ h _ i _ g _ l _

16 p _ e _ s _ n _

17 _ o _ h _ r _

18 s _ y _ a _ k

19 _ p _ o _ b _ l _

20 w _ o _ p _ c _ e _

WATER THE FLOWERS

The names of eleven well-known garden flowers are hidden inside the watering can. See how quickly you can find them. You may use the letters more than once.

LVARCD
TSWFO
PUN
IE

HORNS AND ANTLERS

These animals are a bit confused. They've all been drawn with the wrong horns or antlers! Can you match the right animal with each set of horns or antlers, and put them all out of their misery?

3

4

5

6

ANIMALS ALL

Fill in the letters which we have left blank and you will find the names of 20 animals.

1 _ l _ i _ a _ o _

2 e _ e _ h _ n _

3 _ i _ p _ p _ t _ m _ s

4 r _ i _ o _ e _ o _

5 _ e _ g _ h _ g

6 _ a _ d _ c _ o _

7 b _ f _ a _ o

8 d _ o _ e _ a _ y

9 _ a _ i _ o _

10 c _ i _ m _ n _

11 _ o _ m _ u _ e

12 e _ r _ h _ o _ m

13 _ q _ i _ r _ l

14 g _ r _ f _ e

15 _ l _ w _ _ o _ m

16 g _ a _ s _ o _ p _ r

17 _ a _ m _ r _ e _ d

18 b _ m _ l _ b _ e

19 _ e _ l _ f _ s _

20 l _ o _ a _ d

44

MAKE A BIRD

Take one letter from each bird to find the name of
another. Here is a clue — Marsh and Hen are both
varieties of this bird!

kingfisher —
fieldfare —
redstart —
bittern —
puffin —
heron —
rail —

A DOGGY PUZZLE

There are many different kinds of dog as you will know. We have taken just ten, jumbled up the letters and hidden them in this picture. See how many different kinds you can find.

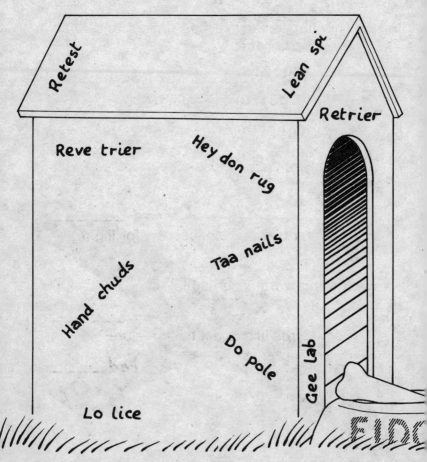

Retest

Lean spi

Retrier

Reve trier

Hey don rug

Taa nails

Hand chuds

Do pole

Gee lab

Lo lice

THEY'RE ALL RED

When you have solved the clues below, put the word RED in front of the answer and you will have the names of ten plants and animals.

1   A senior naval man.

red _ _ _ _ _ _ _

2   This large mammal has antlers and often lives in Scotland.

red _ _ _ _

3   This bushytailed animal can be grey as well as red.

red _ _ _ _ _ _ _ _

4   It has eight legs and is often confused with an insect.

red _ _ _ _ _ _

5   Part of a bird that's necessary for flight.

red _ _ _ _

6   A slang word for grumble.

red _ _ _ _ _ _

7   Some birds like to eat this creature!

red _ _ _ _

IN THE COUNTRY

Inside the sheep you'll find the jumbled names of some other countryside animals. Can you sort them out?

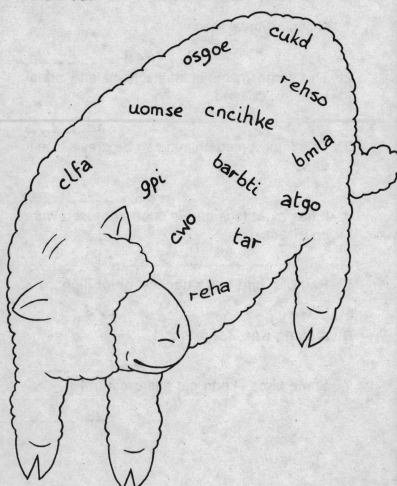

IT'S THE SIZE THAT MATTERS

Add a size to each word given below to make the name of an animal. You might have to add little, big, etc.

1 _ _ _ _ _ **clam** A very large bivalve shellfish.

2 _ _ _ _ _ **blue** A butterfly.

3 _ _ _ _ _ _ **plover** A bird.

4 _ _ _ **horn** A sheep.

5 _ _ _ _ _ _ **crested grebe** Another bird.

6 _ _ _ _ _ **white** Another butterfly.

HIDDEN ANIMALS

You will find a number of mammals hidden in the
square on Mystery Island. Can you discover them
all? Take a pencil and start at the arrow. Then move
up, down, backwards, forwards or even diagonally.
See if you can do this puzzle without taking your
pencil off the paper!

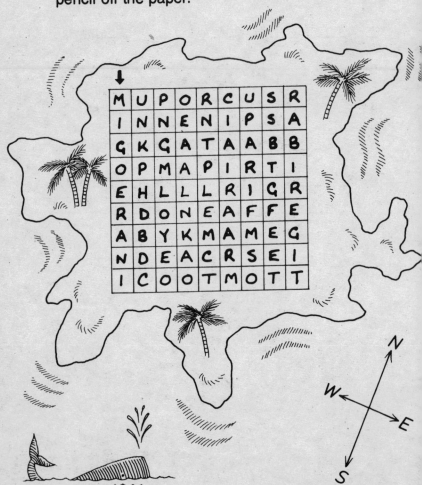

M	U	P	O	R	C	U	S	R
I	N	N	E	N	I	P	S	A
G	K	G	A	T	A	A	B	B
O	P	M	A	P	I	R	T	I
E	H	L	L	L	R	I	G	R
R	D	O	N	E	A	F	F	E
A	B	Y	K	M	A	M	E	G
N	D	E	A	C	R	S	E	I
I	C	O	O	T	M	O	T	T

BEAKS AND BIRDS

Look carefully at these strange birds and you will see that they all have the wrong beaks! Can you match the right beak with the right bird?

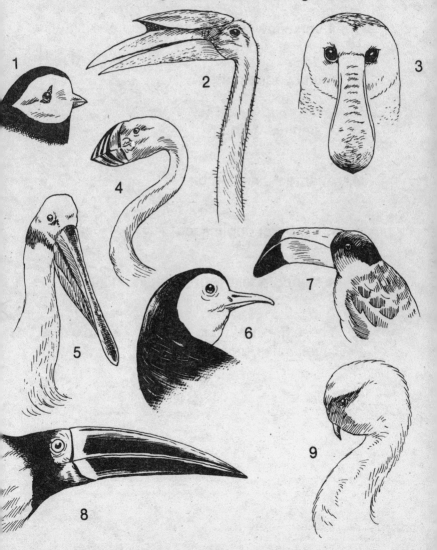

ADD AN ANIMAL

By adding the name of one animal to the letters given below you can make another animal. Clues have been given to help you.

1 A very slow animal.

_ _ _ _ _ _ _ _ shell

2 A tabby for example.

s _ _ _

3 A smoked herring.

s _ _ _ _ _ _

4 A large Australian bird.

l _ _ _ r

5 A hard-working insect.

p _ _ _ her

6 A stubborn fellow or a stupid animal.

b _ _ _

7 These fire-breathing animals may only exist in fairytales.

_ _ _ _ _ _ fly

CHANGE THE X

In the following list put the correct letters in place
of the Xs to make the names of 20 animals.

1 rxxnxcxrxs

2 xxrmxxse

3 dxxedxrx

4 xlxxxaxt

5 dxaxonxly

6 xorixxa

7 hixxoxoxamxs

8 xumxixxbixd

9 kxxgaxoo

10 xxrmoxxt

11 mixlxpexe

12 oxtxpux

13 xrxng-xtxn

14 pxrtxixge

15 xorxoixx

16 poxxupxxe

17 xxrpxixx

18 sxorxixn

19 wxxdpxxkxr

20 xlxixxtxr

A CAT COMES FIRST

Find a one word answer to each sentence below. Then add a 'cat' at the beginning and you'll have made another word.

1 Your mother or father — or any close relative.

cat _ _ _

2 Where money is made.

cat _ _ _ _

3 These are on the side of your head.

cats _ _ _

4 Monkeys swing by these.

cats _ _ _ _

5 This is streamlined for a life in the water.

cat _ _ _ _

6 It has wings and flies.

cat _ _ _ _

HIDDEN FLOWERS

Hidden somewhere in the sentences below are the names of ten flowers. There is one flower in each sentence. Can you spot them all? The first one has been underlined for you. Now try and find the rest.

1   The saucep<u>ans y</u>ou bought are rather small.

2   The panda is your favourite animal.

3   Chopin knew a great deal about music.

4   This shirt has a scorch identical to mine.

5   If you are going down that narrow lane, money is needed to pay the toll.

6   It is possible that the coach is now dropping people for the football match.

7   When the volcano erupted without warning it was a disaster for everyone.

8   See if you can get a picture of the rhinoceros entering the water.

9   Get Dad and Eli on the next flight.

10   Keep a tape on your video ready for the next film.

ALL THAT GLITTERS

All the plants and animals in this section have either 'gold' or 'golden' in their names. We have given you a few clues!

1 Britain's smallest bird.

gold _ _ _ _ _

2 A duck.

golden _ _ _

3 A garden and wild flower.

golden _ _ _

4 A bird which eats seeds.

gold _ _ _ _ _

5 Common finned animal often kept at home.

gold _ _ _ _

6   This plant gives its name to a fairytale character.

gold _ _ _ _ _ _

7   A bird which builds an eyrie.

golden _ _ _ _ _

8   This small mammal stores food in its cheeks.

golden _ _ _ _ _ _ _

9   A furry mammal well-known for burrowing.

golden _ _ _ _

10   Some are game birds.

golden _ _ _ _ _ _ _ _

AN ANIMAL SAYING

Find the right way through the muddled letters below and you will end up with a well-known proverb.

Take a pencil and start at the arrow. Then move up, down, backwards, forwards or diagonally, without taking the pencil off the paper.

E	H	E	H
S	O	T	R
R	O	E	O
D	N	E	F
P	T	B	T
U	T	C	R
T	H	E	A

→ (points to the D in row 4)

WHERE DO THEY LIVE?

Can you match a word from the left-hand column with a word from the right-hand column and find homes for these ten animals?

ANIMAL	HOME
1 Blackbird	sty
2 Bee	drey
3 Otter	sett
4 Fox	stable
5 Squirrel	earth
6 Badger	holt
7 Hare	nest
8 Pig	hive
9 Rabbit	form
10 Horse	warren

BEARS ABOUT

Jumbled in the bear below are the names of six other bears. See how quickly you can unscramble the letters to find their names.

plora

zlriyzg

dkokai

nsu

lbcak

wornb

BEAUTIFUL BUTTERFLIES

If you can answer the questions below, you will have the names of five well-known butterflies.

1   You should, almost certainly, see two of these in this sentence.

2   He's not really a communist naval man.

3   Doesn't really refer to a little loaf of bread.

4   Not the covering for a little reptile.

5   The fuel of hell fire?

STRANGE ANIMALS

These animals look rather strange because they're all wearing the wrong coats! See if you can match the right coat with the right animal.

3

4

5

6

HIDDEN INSECTS

Hidden in the sentences below are the names of ten insects. There is one insect in each sentence. See if you can find them all. The first sentence has been done for you.

1 His <u>cap hides</u> his short hair.

2 The minimum items are listed.

3 You must be ever so careful with the gas.

4 Sugar beet leads us to sugar.

5 I hear wigwams are for Indians.

6 It is easy to baffle Alfred with science.

7 If you place winged insects in the cage they will be safe.

8 I'm sure Oslo uses green buses.

9 If it was possible, Mike would be here.

10 You should farm other crops to make a profit.

CODED BIRDS

The figures in the bird below look a bit like a problem for a mathematician. They are quite simple really. Just put a letter in place of each number and you'll find the names of ten birds.
A = 1, B = 2 and so on.

1   20, 8, 18, 21, 19, 8

2   19, 16, 1, 18, 18, 15, 23

3   15, 19, 16, 18, 5, 25

4   19, 23, 1, 12, 12, 15, 23

5   2, 12, 21, 5, 20, 9, 20

6   25, 5, 12, 12, 15, 23, 8, 1, 13, 13, 5, 18

7   16, 1, 18, 20, 18, 9, 4, 7, 5

8   18, 15, 2, 9, 14

9   3, 18, 15, 23

10   18, 5, 4, 23, 9, 14, 7

GROUPS OF ANIMALS

Most animals have group names. There are twenty of these names dotted about the page. Can you pick the right one to complete the following sentences?

1 A _ _ _ _ _ _ of geese.

2 A _ _ _ _ _ of sheep.

3 A _ _ _ _ _ of cattle.

4 A _ _ _ _ _ of lions.

5 A _ _ _ _ _ _ of bears.

6 A _ _ _ _ of hares.

7 A _ _ _ _ _ _ of pigs.

8 A _ _ _ _ of horses.

9 A _ _ _ _ _ of flies.

10 A _ _ _ _ _ _ of doves.

11 A _ _ _ _ of wolves.

12 A _ _ _ _ of buffaloes.

13 A _ _ _ _ _ _ of whales.

14 A _ _ _ _ of badgers.

15 A _ _ _ _ of rabbits.

swarm *stud* *flock* *litter* *nest* *flight* *gaggle* *sleuth* *pride* *pack* *herd* *drove* *down* *school* *cete*

MOUNTAIN ANIMALS

This mountain goat has a number of other animal names jumbled up inside it. They are all mountain animals, too. Can you work them out?

rabe

pear lod

flow

cajlak

bixe

ayk

TREE QUIZ

Test your knowledge of trees with this quiz. See how quickly you can find all 20 answers.

1 The flowers of this tree are often called candles.

2 Known as the rowan, what is this tree's other name?

3 This tree has the name of a girl and its catkins are called lamb's tails.

4 You might go to one kind of this tree if you wanted wood for a cricket bat.

5 Timber cut from this evergreen tree, which has poisonous berries, was used to make long bows. What is its name?

6 Which tree produces acorns in autumn?

7 Which tree, often found in cities, sheds its bark when it gets worn?

8 Wych and English are types of which tree?

9 Which tree has cigar-shaped, black buds through the winter?

10 Brought to England from north of the border, this tree is the only British pine. What is it called?

11 Which is the only evergreen tree in Britain to lose its needles in winter?

12 The berries of this hedgerow shrub are known as haws.

13 The hip is the wild fruit of which shrub?

14 If you look on the Canadian national flag which tree leaf will you find?

15 The colour of the bark gives this tree part of its name.

16 Pigs used to feed on mast in the New Forest. Which tree does mast come from?

17 This particular evergreen comes from Lebanon.

18 Which tree is often associated with ivy — especially at Christmas?

19 Why does the weeping willow have this name?

20 This tree likes its feet (roots) in water. What is its name?

ANIMAL CROSSWORD

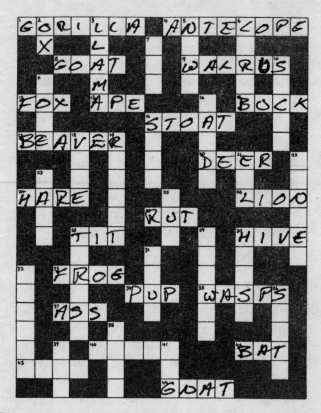

Clues

Across: 1 Large ape. 4 An animal with antlers. 8 Nanny, maybe. 9 Similar to a sea lion, but heavier! 12 Sly animal with a bushy tail. 13 One kind lives on Gibraltar. 15 Male deer. 16 Sometimes confused with the weasel. 17 Builds dams. 20 Can be both red and fallow. 24 Mad as a March . . . . . 26 Often called 'King of the Jungle'. 27 The mating season in deer. 28 Blue, great, coal, etc. 30 Where the bees make honey. 33 Spawns in spring. 34 A kind of dog. 35 Black and yellow insects. 37 A horse-like animal, but with longer ears. 40 The stone where a thrush cracks open snail shells. 42 Hangs upside down when sleeping. 43 A type of duck. 44 A biting insect.

Down: 2 The _ _ and the ass. 3 South American beast of burden. 5 Great Crested perhaps? 6 Related to the lemur and lives in trees. 7 Sea fish. 10 The serpent in the Garden of Eden. 11 Lives in tunnels underground. 14 Giant and red _ _ _ _ _. 16 Animal that lives in the sea. 18 This one makes holes in river banks. 19 Where a lot live together it's a warren. 21 Slippery fish? 22 A sea bird (likes to eat a lot.) 23 Female horse. 25 The underground tunnel of a vole or mole, for example. 28 The blackbird is one and so are the redwing and fieldfare. 29 An insect with pincers. 30 Originally used to pull the plough. 31 Slimey creature without a shell. 32 These black and white coastal birds breed at Minsmere in Suffolk. 36 Slow-moving mammal. 38 A bird — could be a bit tied up! 39 A letter of the alphabet and a bird. 41 Most animals walk on more than one.

WILD FLOWERS

See how many of the wild flowers you can identify from the drawings below.

BIRD SAYINGS

We have left out some words from the sayings below. All the missing words are associated with, or have the names of, birds. See if you can fill in all the blanks.

1 Up with the _ _ _ _ .

2 A _ _ _ _ in the hand is worth two in the bush.

3 As the _ _ _ _ flies.

4 Don't count your _ _ _ _ _ _ _ _ before they hatch.

5 What is sauce for the _ _ _ _ _ is sauce for the _ _ _ _ _ _ .

6 As wise as an _ _ _ .

7 The early _ _ _ _ catches the worm.

8 Birds of a _ _ _ _ _ _ _ flock together.

9 As bald as a _ _ _ _ .

10 Don't put all your _ _ _ _ in one basket.

ANIMALS OVERSEAS

How much do you know about animals in other parts of the world? Try this quiz to test your knowledge.

1 This East African bird sticks its head in the sand. Which one is it and how fast does it travel when running?

2 In which country are budgerigars found in the wild?

3 Which mammals are specially associated with Gibraltar?

4 It lives in South Africa and is known as the 'earth pig'. Which animal is it?

5 Name the bear which lives on Arctic ice floes.

6 This mammal hunts in packs and is thought to be the ancestor of our modern dogs. What is its name?

7   The hippopotamus lives in Africa. What does its name mean?

8   The kiwi lives in New Zealand. How did it get its name?

9   What is the correct name for the North American reindeer?

10 The 'goat antelope' is found in European mountain ranges. We use its skin for cleaning purposes. What is its real name?

11 Which is the only type of marsupial living in America?

12 This mammal, which only lives in the rain forests of Central Africa, is the only living relative of the giraffe. What is its name?

13 Which large ape has a name which means 'jungle man'? Where does it live?

14 Australians call this bird the 'laughing jackass'. What is its proper name?

15 Which North American beetle is a pest because it attacks potato crops?

16 The horn on the African rhino is not horn. What is it made of?

17 Amongst birds, what distinction does the Andean condor have?

18 This Australian marsupial is sometimes known as the 'Australian bear'. What is it called and what is its main source of food?

19 Solenodons sleep in burrows, hollow trees and caves. They are only found on two islands. Which are they?

20 This animal, which lives in Africa, has a striped body and takes its name from a type of drum. Which animal is it?

A FISHY PROBLEM

There are some letters in the squares below to help you solve this fishy problem. All the answers are names of fish and, if you fill in the letters correctly, you will have the name of another fish across the middle.

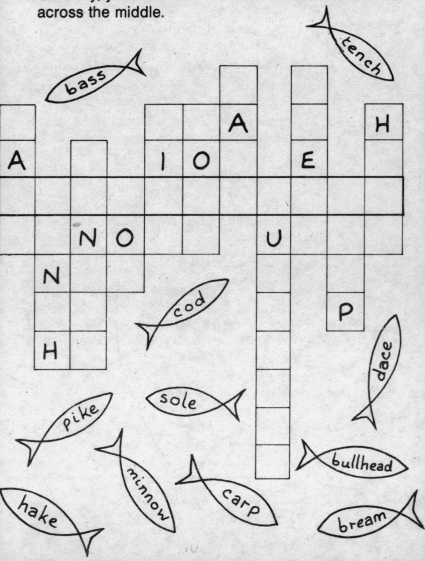

DISCOVER THE DEER

The picture below hides the names of seven different types of deer. Re-arrange the letters to find out what they are.

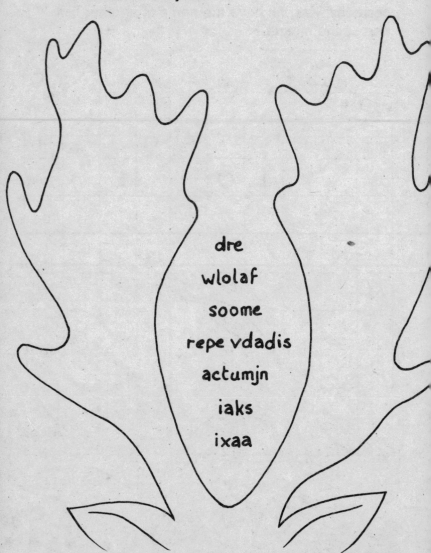

dre

wlolaf

soome

repe vdadis

actumjn

iaks

ixaa

ANIMAL WORD SQUARE

There are a lot of animal names hidden in the
square below. Some are written upwards, some
downwards, and some from side to side. How
many can you find?

B	R	E	I	N	D	E	E	R	C	X	P	Q	A	A	B	E
L	M	N	O	P	Q	S	A	M	P	A	L	L	I	R	O	G
L	P	B	S	A	L	A	M	A	N	D	E	R	C	F	R	E
A	M	L	T	R	E	Q	O	L	L	I	D	A	M	R	A	H
M	H	G	O	H	L	M	Q	S	R	A	T	S	B	E	N	L
A	D	N	A	P	T	N	A	I	G	S	B	B	R	C	G	A
P	P	U	T	O	R	O	L	B	I	R	I	C	A	G	U	F
X	B	I	D	L	E	O	P	A	R	D	E	H	E	I	T	I
H	J	G	I	E	G	H	S	T	A	C	B	F	B	H	A	J
A	I	O	E	M	D	I	U	C	F	G	J	B	N	D	N	N
T	F	K	L	M	A	E	M	Z	F	H	A	L	W	G	I	M
E	J	B	E	I	B	E	A	V	E	R	L	I	O	N	L	S
E	H	L	R	N	I	H	T	I	G	K	L	L	R	J	R	U
H	Y	D	R	G	T	C	O	F	B	I	I	P	B	G	N	P
C	H	J	I	G	Z	F	P	K	R	Y	H	T	N	T	O	Y
E	E	S	U	O	M	R	O	D	A	M	C	X	O	F	I	T
K	D	L	Q	K	H	I	P	G	R	X	N	E	O	H	L	A
E	I	O	S	A	H	P	P	I	J	L	I	R	C	I	A	L
G	K	B	T	P	D	F	I	Z	B	K	H	E	A	G	E	P
B	H	K	E	I	T	R	H	I	N	O	C	E	R	O	S	R

LEAVES, FRUITS AND SEEDS

Many common trees can be identified from their leaves and by the fruits or seeds which they produce. Can you pair up these leaves with their fruits and seeds?

WEATHER PERMITTING

The names of the animals in this puzzle all have some connection with weather — thunder, gale, storm and so on.

1 A sting in the tail from whichever direction it's blowing.

2 A two-winged insect accompanied by lightning.

3 A spotted cat with cold connections.

4 A butterfly whose first name suggests overcast conditions.

5 This feathered creature certainly gets wet.

6 This fish could be seen when rain comes with sunshine.

7 Accompanies thunder for this insect.

8 This seabird is in for unpleasant weather.

9 This mammal welcomes the warmth.

10 It seems like the wind will be up for this insect.

TAKE THE LETTERS

First find the answer to each clue. Then, using the numbers at the end of each answer, take out the letters you will need to use. Write the letters out in order on page 84 and you will have an animal proverb!

1 A beast of burden.

_ _ _ (1)

2 A common garden bird whose name has a dark colour in it.

_ _ _ _ _ _ _ _ _ (6,7,8,9)

3 This bird can be green, chaff or gold.

_ _ _ _ _ (2,3)

4 A member of the cat family — the leopard!

_ _ _ _ _ _ _ (4,5,6)

5 A large sea mammal. One species is called 'blue'.

_ _ _ _ _ (2,3)

6 A Chinese official gave his name to this duck.

_ _ _ _ _ _ _ _ (3,4)

7   You might kiss under this at Christmas!

_ _ _ _ _ _ _ _ (2,3)

8   A large sea fish with a long and pointed upper jaw.

_ _ _ _ _ _ _ _ _ (2,3,4)

9   A very slow, tree-climbing mammal

_ _ _ _ _ (4,5)

10 Wild ones live in warrens, tame ones in hutches!

_ _ _ _ _ _ (6)

11 This burrowing animal looks like a small bear, but has a pouch. It lives in Southern Australia and Tasmania.

_ _ _ _ _ _ (1,2)

12 House and sand are both types of this bird. The house variety builds its nest under the eaves.

_ _ _ _ _ _ (5,6)

13 The only mammals that can fly!

_ _ _ _ (3)

14 A short name for a chicken.

_ _ _ (1,2)

15   This small, tree-climbing mammal has large eyes and ears and a long bushy tail. It is related to the loris and the lemur.

_ _ _ _ _ _ _ _ (1,2,3,4)

_ _ _ _ _ _ _ _ _ _ _ _ _

_ _ _ _ _ _ _ _ _ _ _ _ _ _ _ _ .

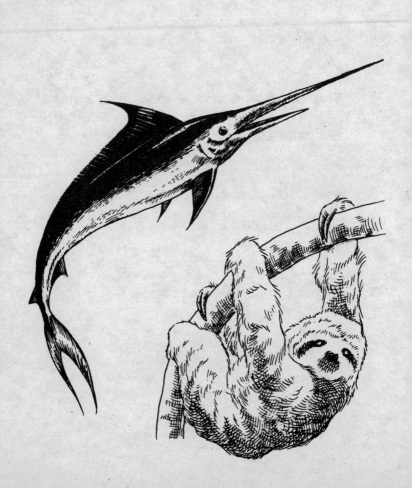

MISSING VOWELS

We've left vowels out of the following words. Fill each space below with A, E, I, O or U, and you'll have the names of ten animals.

1 _ l _ p h _ n t

2 s h _ _ r w _ t _ r

3 b _ _ v _ r

4 k _ n g _ r _ _

5 p _ n t _ _ l

6 d _ r m _ _ s _

7 r h _ n _ c _ r _ s

8 s _ l _ m _ n d _ r

9 c h _ m _ l _ _ n

10 h _ r t _ b _ _ s t

MORE BIRDS

The centre word has been filled in. Can you fill in the other blanks to discover the names of the rest of the birds? We have given you some clues.

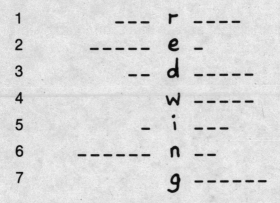

1   _ _ _   r   _ _ _ _
2   _ _ _ _ _   e   _
3   _ _   d   _ _ _ _ _ _
4   w   _ _ _ _ _ _
5   _   i   _ _ _
6   _ _ _ _ _ _   n   _ _
7   g   _ _ _ _ _ _

Solve the two parts of each question to find two words. Put the two words together and you'll have the name of a bird!

1   Twinkle, twinkle little _ _ _ _ and a kind of heather.

2   An open piece of land and another name for chicken.

3   A traffic light colour and a beginning.

4   A cover for a bald head and a very long period of time.

5   Found in oranges and a place for mining coal.

6   The name of an animal that is affected by the colour red, and a seed-eating bird.

7   A dull colour and something you might do to pipes to stop them freezing in winter.

ANIMAL RIDDLE

Work out the clue in each line of this riddle. Then you'll find the letters that make up the name of a boney-plated animal.

My first is in lizard and also in snake.

My second in rudd but never in hake.

My third in monkey but not in ape.

My fourth in buffalo, as well as in cape.

My fifth in dandelion but not in flower.

My sixth in bird yet not in bower.

My seventh in piglet but not in sow.

My eighth in milk but never in cow.

My ninth in mouse and also in stoat.

My whole has a very hard-plated coat.

HIDDEN BIRDS

Hidden in the sentence below are the names of ten birds. There is one in each sentence. See how many you can find. The first sentence has been done for you.

1   Nicholas <u>wants</u> a record player.

2   The star lingers long in the sky.

3   This is her only dress.

4   The kit ensures good results.

5   The blank notices do not give good instructions.

6   Put the lid over the paint can.

7   This site always has good orchids.

8   The saw renders the wood unfit for painting.

9   He's the biggest crook I know.

10 We will use grass with rushes for our display.

PLACE NAMES

The answers to the clues below are all either place names or are associated with places — e.g. Yorkshire, Welsh, etc. Add your answer to the word at the end of each clue, and find the name of a plant or animal.

1 A borough in north London.

_ _ _ _ _ *goose*

2 A part of south London.

_ _ _ _ _ _ _ _ _ _ *beauty*

3 An American state.

_ _ _ _ _ _ _ _ *beetle*

4 The capital of France.

herb _ _ _ _ _

5 Britain's capital city.

_ _ _ _ _ _ *pride*

6 A part of North America.

_ _ _ _ _ _ *goose*

7 Someone who comes from one of the continents.

_ _ _ _ _ _ _ *elephant*

8 Of the Isle of Man.

$----$ cat

9 Islands off America famous for their wildlife.

$----------$ tortoise

10 A part of India.

$------$ tiger

11 It must be cold here!

$------$ tern

12 People from a country to the west of Spain.

$----------$ man-o-war

13 People living north of the English border.

$-----$ pine

14 Its capital is Oslo.

$------$ spruce

COME FLY WITH US

Take the answers to all the clues below, add the word **fiy** and you will have the animal or insect we are looking for.

1   A maiden, but not in distress.

$- - - - - -$ **fly**

2   A fiery monster.

$- - - - - -$ **fly**

3   A British tree.

$- - - - -$ **fly**

4   It lifts heavy weights.

$- - - - -$ **fly**

5   What many of us live in.

$- - - - -$ **fly**

6   We use the milk from cows to make this.

$- - - - - -$ **fly**

7   You could cut wood with this.

$- - -$ **fly**

8   It is said to be the merry month.

$- - -$ **fly**

9   A four-legged animal whose young is a foal.

$- - - - -$ **fly**

ANIMAL RIDDLE

Work out the clue in each line of this riddle. You should then find eight letters to make the name of a small animal.

My first is in birch and also in beech.

My second in horse and also in leech.

My third in donkey, but not in foal.

My fourth in herring but not in shoal.

My fifth in green but not in grass.

My sixth in hake but not in bass.

My seventh in owl and also in hoot.

My last in grouse, but not in coot.

My whole is a very prickly animal.

THE NAME'S THE SAME

The one-word answer to each question below is also the name of an animal. Remember, birds and fish are animals too!

1   You do this when you drink.

    _ _ _ _ _ _ _

2   Certainly you would be quick.

    _ _ _ _ _

3   A flag or decoration.

    _ _ _ _ _ _ _

4   A rather funny prank.

    _ _ _ _ _ _ _

5   Someone who sings.

    _ _ _ _ _ _ _

6   Slang for someone who is rather silly.

    _ _ _ _ _ _

7   A brave nurse in the Crimean War.

    _ _ _ _ _ _ _ _ _ _

8   A famous magician in Camelot.

    _ _ _ _ _ _

9   St Paul's Cathedral is his masterpiece.

    _ _ _ _

10 To do something as a pastime.

_ _ _ _ _

11 A train travels along these.

_ _ _ _

12 You might use this to make a hole.

_ _ _ _ _

13 You can do this when there is frozen water.

_ _ _ _ _

14 A summer game in Britain.

_ _ _ _ _ _ _

15 To grumble.

_ _ _ _ _ _

16 A greedy person.

_ _ _

17 A type of footwear.

_ _ _ _

18 An undersized person.

_ _ _ _ _ _

19 To pester someone.

_ _ _ _ _ _

20 You use this to play table tennis.

_ _ _

HIDDEN FRUIT

Hidden in the sentences below are the names of ten fruits. There is one hidden in each sentence. The first sentence has been done for you.

1   You ca<u>me, long</u> time, no see.

2   John also lives near me in town.

3   I think we will ban a national visit.

4   I figure the next bus will be here soon.

5   We'll reap plenty for our labours.

6   The dried pea changes shape when soaked in water.

7   I have little money, but I am happy.

8   To get practice in we'll have to change to range shooting.

9   Ploughing rapes the countryside destroying its beauty.

10 The chimp lumps all his food together.

IN THE COUNTRY

Take a countryside word from the left-hand column and add it to a word from the right-hand column. You will then have the name of a plant or animal.

hedge	slip
pond	cup
field	sparrow
butter	chestnut
cow	keeper
horse	skater
fox	creeper
milk	weed
tree	fare
gate	glove

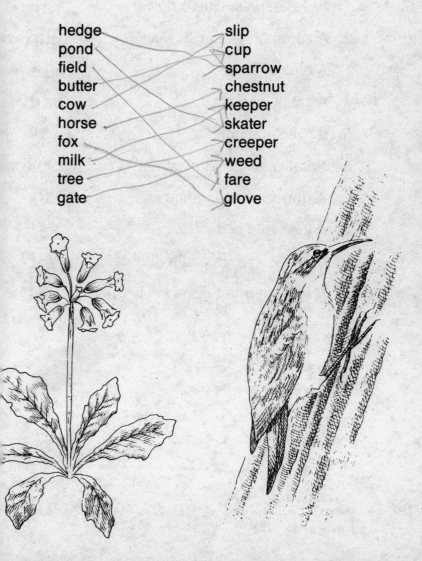

FROM BEGINNING TO END

The end of each answer is already given. All you
have to do is use the clues to find the beginning!
See how quickly you can find the answers.

1   A well-known Dutch flower.   *lip*

2   A common yellow flower.   *cup*

3   A bird of prey.   *gle*

4   A small mammal.   *use*

5   It lives in a holt.   *ter*

6   Britain's smallest mammal.   *rew*

7   A flower of springtime.   *dil*

8   It lives in a sett.   *ger*

9   It has long ears and a little tail.   *bit*

10 May be red but more likely grey.   *rel*

11 He may sleep during winter. **hog**

12 Found in the seas around the coast. **imp**

13 Often called Polly for some reason. **rot**

14 Britain's only poisonous snake. **per**

15 The African variety has larger ears and tusks than its Indian cousin. **ant**

16 Usually builds its nest under the eaves. **low**

17 A rare bird that breeds in Scotland. **rey**

18 A well-known fish. **mon**

19 A winter bird visitor. **ing**

20 Can be a billy or a nanny. **at**

ON THE SEASHORE

In the puzzle below you will find the names of seven different things which can be found on the seashore. Starting from the arrow and moving upwards, downwards, from side to side, or diagonally, try to find them all — without lifting your pencil off the paper!

C	P	I	R	L	L	A	E
R	M	H	S	Y	O	H	S
A	S	S	E	L	U	L	L
B	O	U	S	A	G	G	N
C	C	M	E	W	E	R	I
K	L	E	E	E	D	H	R

ANOTHER NAME FOR IT

By solving the clues below you will have the names of eight animals. For example, a type of drum is a bongo — and a bongo is the name of an antelope. See if you can work them out.

1 You can wash yourself with one of these.

Sponge

2 A brown spot on the body.

mole

3 Elizabeth I wore one of these round her neck.

Lace

4 In the sky, this is usually attached to string.

———

5 Something for a bird to stand on.

perch

6 One who sings low down in a choir.

———

7 Part of the foot or the bottom of a shoe.

sole

8 A shaft of sunlight.

——

WHITER THAN WHITE

Add the word **white** at the front of each answer and you will have the names of ten plants and animals.

1   Join the navy and reach a high rank

2   This is used to attract fish.

3   A large piece of wood which can often be seen in old houses.

4   The opposite of back.

5   This is the best way to travel from Britain to Australia.

6   Part of the body where the Adam's apple is found.

7   Darwin called it 'nature's ploughman'.

8   One of nature's strongest insects.

9   Fins are a feature.

10   This plant does not sting.

HOOK, LINE AND SINKER

Starting from the arrow, and moving upwards, downwards, or from side to side, see how quickly you can find the eight fish hidden in the square (without lifting your pencil off the paper).

					↓
L	E	E	K	C	S
B	O	T	L	I	T
R	A	B	E	A	I
U	C	K	P	L	C
T	R	E	D	D	E
H	C	P	O	A	H
M	O	N	C	K	P
L	A	S	E	K	I

TWO TIMING

There are two clues and two answers for each of these questions. The two animal or plant answers are hidden in the jumbled word. The letters are all in order!

1 Find the mammal and also a rare bird.

BUOFSFPRALEYO

2 The butterfly is found in the Norfolk Broads and so is the bird.

BSWIALTTLOEWTRAINL

3 A dazzling insect as well as a reptile.

GRDRAAGONSSFSNLAKYE

4 This web-footed animal feeds on these fish.

OSATLMTEONR

5 One of the first flowers of spring, and a member of the thrush family which comes to us in winter.

FCIEOLLTDSFOFOARTE

6 Found together where dead animals lie.

JVUACLKTUAREL

7 The largest land mammal and the largest mammal. Elephant

ELWEPHHAALNET

8 A common wild flower and a common tree.

BHOUTRSETERCCHESUTNPUT

9 Two plants which flower in spring.

CSNROOWDCRUSOP

10 They are both Australian marsupials.

KKOANAGLAROAO

OCCUPATIONS

Look at the two lists of words below. Put the right words from each list together and you'll find the names of ten hard-working animals.

angler	sailor
shepherd's	admiral
red	fish
butcher	beetle
soldier	purse
cardinal	ant
engraver	fish
by-the-wind	beetle
reeve's	pheasant
archer	bird

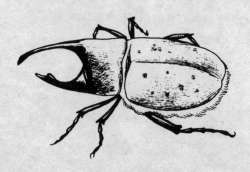

HIDDEN BIRDS

Hidden in the square are the names of six birds. Starting from the arrow and moving upwards, downwards, from side to side, or diagonally, keep your pencil on the paper and you will quickly name them all.

R	W	R	A	I	M
E	O	R	P	S	T
D	S	H	S	E	L
K	N	A	G	T	H
L	P	I	N	I	R
V	O	L	N	W	U
E	S	R	G	D	S
R	T	A	E	R	H

ANIMAL SAYINGS

We have illustrated some animal sayings below. See if you can work out what they are.

1

2

3

4

5

NATURE ALPHABET

Now test your knowledge of nature by making a list each of trees, birds and mammals. See if you can name one for each letter of the alphabet. How many spaces are you left with?

	TREES	BIRDS	MAMMALS
A	AShtree		
B	Beachtree	bull finch	Badoon
C	chestnut	chaffinch	chimpanzie
D			
E			
F			
G		graytit	gorila
H			
I			
J			
K			
L			
M			
N			

	TREES	BIRDS	MAMMALS
O	Oak tree		
P			
Q			
R			
S			
T			
U			
V			
W			
X			
Y		yellow hammer	
Z			

TWENTY WAYS TO HELP OUR PLANET

1 Take bottles to the bottle bank for recycling.

2 Make sure your family use 'ozone-friendly' products.

3 Always use both sides of any paper you are writing on.

4 Keep envelopes and re-use them with sticky labels.

5 Suggest a 'Care for the Envirinment Day' at school, or at your club or church.

6 Plant some wild flowers in your garden to attract bees and butterflies. You can do this in tubs and window boxes if you don't have a garden, but ask your parents first!

7 Save all your table scraps in winter and make 'puddings' to feed to the birds.

8 Put up a bird table. Attach one to the window ledge or wall if you don't have a garden. Ask an adult to help you.

9 Grow some vegetables using natural fertilizers.

10 Join a local young people's group like *The Young Ornithologists' Club* or *Watch*. You will be able to go to meetings and learn more about nature.

11 Save your newspapers for recycling.

12 If you know a piece of wasteland close to your home or school, try to get people interested in setting up a little park there.

13 If you have a suitable garden, ask if you can make a pond.

14 Always close doors behind you, especially in winter. This helps prevent heat loss. Don't forget to turn off lights to save energy.

15 Never drop litter — and suggest to your friends that you all pick up any you see. Have a 'litter pick', or get involved with *Operation Springclean*.

16 Look for, and collect, discarded bottles. They can become traps for small creatures. Take them to the bottle bank.

17 Save foil, which can be recycled.

18 Put up nestboxes for birds and bats in your garden.

19 It takes more 'energy' to produce meat than plants. Eat less meat and more organically grown vegetables.

20 Go by foot rather than by car. If you must travel try to use the train or bus. This helps cut down on pollution.

Some Useful Addresses:

Countryside Commission, John Dower House, Crescent Place, Cheltenham, Gloucestershire GL50 3RA

The Young Ornithologists' Club, The Lodge, Sandy, Bedfordshire SG19 2DL

Watch, Royal Society for Nature Conservation, The Green, Nettleham, Lincoln LN2 2NR

Operation Springclean is organised by local councils in association with the *Tidy Britain Group.*

AND SO TO THE END

For the final puzzle, see if you can name all the plants and animals below. They all begin with the letters X, Y or Z.

ANSWERS

Animals and Plants (page 5)

Harebell; puss moth; peacock butterfly; coltsfoot; catmint; horsefly; froghopper; sparrowhawk; sow thistle; anteater.

Find the Minibeasts (page 6)

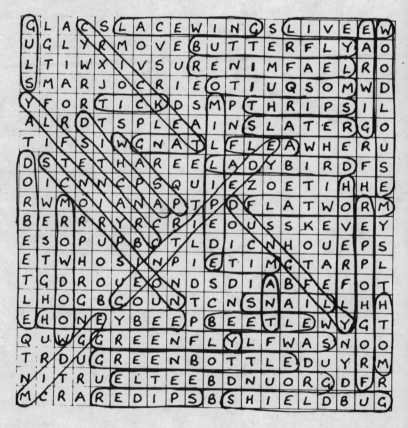

Berries (page 8)
1 Elderberry; 2 cranberry; 3 snowberry; 4 blackberry; 5 strawberry; 6 bilberry; 7 gooseberry; 8 raspberry; 9 mulberry; 10 blueberry.

Find the Young (page 9)
1 Cub; 2 lamb; 3 puppy; 4 foal; 5 gosling; 6 chick; 7 piglet; 8 cygnet; 9 calf; 10 leveret; 11 fawn; 12 kitten.

Well Hidden (page 10)
1 Frog; 2 goat; 3 bear; 4 hare; 5 lion; 6 seal; 7 tiger; 8 cow; 9 toad; 10 rat; 11 horse; 12 pica; 13 beaver; 14 dog; 15 lemur; 16 monkey; 17 otter; 18 ass; 19 cat; 20 sloth.

Oddbodland Birds (page 12)
1 Fieldfare; 2 blackbird; 3 starling; 4 osprey; 5 robin; 6 redshank; 7 oystercatcher; 8 redwing; 9 gannet; 10 albatross.

Animal Sayings (page 13)
1 Cat; 2 mouse; 3 pig; 4 wolf; 5 horse's; 6 fox; 7 lamb; 8 wolf/sheep's; 9 bee; 10 ox.

Penguins (page 14)
Adele; emperor; king; gentoo; rockhopper; humboldt; royal.

Monkeys and Apes (page 15)
Gorilla; orang-utan; baboon; chimpanzee; lemur.

Against the Wall (page 16)
1 Wall brown; 2 wall creeper; 3 wallflower; 4 wallpepper; 5 wallrue.

Muddled Animals (page 17)
1 Giraffe; 2 tortoise; 3 monkey; 4 sea lion; 5 dormouse; 6 otter; 7 beaver; 8 elephant; 9 gorilla; 10 panda.

Heads and Tails (page 18)
1 Thrush; 2 sparrow; 3 mallard; 4 monkey; 5 condor; 6 agouti; 7 bighorn; 8 bittern; 9 abalone; 10 alpaca.

Fruit Salad (page 19)
1 Apple; 2 plum; 3 pear; 4 passion fruit; 5 cherry; 6 orange; 7 grapefruit; **new fruit**: apricot.

On the Farm (page 20)
cat; sheep; donkey; foal; mare; bull; turkey; lamb; horse; sheepdog.

Books and Films (page 21)
1 Wind in the Willows; 2 Ring of Bright Water; 3 Tarka the Otter; 4 Black Beauty; 5 The Living Desert; 6 Serengeti Shall Not Die; 7 The Running Foxes; 8 The Jungle Book; 9 Call of the Wild; 10 Watership Down.

Parts of the Body (page 22)
1 Coltsfoot; 2 mistletoe; 3 hairstreak butterfly; 4 oxlip; 5 oxeye daisy; 6 earwig; 7 heartsease; 8 liverwort; 9 adderstongue; 10 daddy longlegs; 11 millers thumb; 12 whitethroat; 13 bladderwort; 14 lady's fingers; 15 lung fish; 16 kidney vetch; 17 snail; 18 bloodworm.

Birds in a Muddle (page 24)
1 Tawny owl; 2 marsh warbler; 3 goldcrest; 4 spotted flycatcher; 5 tree creeper; 6 greenfinch; 7 pied wagtail; 8 redshank; 9 sand martin; 10 rock pipit; 11 little gull; 12 common tern (or little tern and common gull); 13 hen harrier; 14 corn crake; 15 wood sandpiper (or marsh

sandpiper & wood warbler); 16 house sparrow; 17 collared dove; 18 reed bunting; 19 black grouse; 20 grey plover.

A Fruity Problem (page 25)
Apple; melon; plum; lemon; grape; raspberry; greengage; orange; peach; apricot; cherry.
New fruit: pomegranate.

Ants in the Answers (page 26)
1 Elephant; 2 anteater; 3 giant panda; 4 panther; 5 Canterbury bell.

Creatures of the Waters (page 27)
1 Seal; 2 sea lion; 3 walrus; 4 porpoise; 5 whale; 6 otter; 7 beaver; 8 dolphin; 9 shark; 10 ray.

Riddled Birds (page 28)
1 Redstart; 2 razor-bill; 3 nightingale; 4 puffin; 5 knot; 6 bittern; 7 rock dove; 8 tern; 9 swift; 10 stork.

Wildlife in Danger (page 30)
1 Wryneck; 2 dormouse; 3 blue whale; 4 bittern; 5 ruff; 6 snowy owl; 7 New Zealand; 8 Scottish wild cat; 9 orchids; 10 Tasmanian devil; 11 square-lipped — from the Dutch language; 12 African elephant; 13 springbok; 14 goose; 15 early morning and early evening; 16 Dartford; 17 large blue butterfly; 18 smooth snake; adder (also known as the viper), and grass snake; 19 barn owl; 20 red kite.

The Name Game (page 32)
1 Sweet william; 2 jack-by-the-hedge; 3 pearlwort; 4 herb robert; 5 lily-of-the-valley; 6 jacob's ladder; 7 wild rose; 8 douglas fir; 9 creeping jenny; 10 bog myrtle; 11 ground ivy; 12 dog violet; 13 ox-eye daisy; 14 stinking bob; 15 field pansy.

Add a Word (page 33)
1 Fox; 2 mink; 3 stag; 4 snipe; 5 acorn; 6 panther; 7 teal; 8 goat; 9 badger.

In the Bible (page 34)
Sheep; mule; lamb; ram; kangaroo; elephant; goat; calf; donkey; camel; fox; unicorn; ass; lion; badger.

Bird Riddle (page 35)
Sparrow

Animal Outlines (page 36)
1 Elephant; 2 kangaroo; 3 tiger; 4 ostrich; 5 hippopotamus; 6 goose; 7 whale; 8 bear; 9 deer; 10 rabbit.

Hidden Flowers (page 38)
Heather; dandelion; clover; chickweed; poppy; buttercup; ivy.

Crafty Creatures (page 39)
1 Cat; 2 cavy; 3 camel; 4 coyote; 5 cheetah; 6 chipmunk; 7 crocodile.

Spaces for Birds (page 40)
1 Herring gull; 2 blackbird; 3 starling; 4 kingfisher; 5 albatross; 6 shearwater; 7 chaffinch; 8 cormorant; 9 partridge; 10 dabchick; 11 guillemot; 12 flycatcher; 13 kittiwake; 14 lapwing; 15 nightingale; 16 pheasant; 17 pochard; 18 skylark; 19 spoonbill; 20 woodpecker.

Water the Flowers (page 41)
Carnation; iris; lavender; lilac; lupin; rose; tulip; daffodil; wallflower; crocus; snowdrop.

Horns and Antlers (page 42)
1 (Bison) needs the horns of 4; 2 (red deer) needs the horns of 1; 3 (water buffalo) needs the horns of 2; 4 (musk ox) needs the horns of 5; 5 (reindeer) needs the horns of 6; 6 (rhinoceros) needs the horns of 3.

Animals All (page 44)
1 Alligator; 2 elephant; 3 hippopotamus; 4 rhinoceros; 5 hedgehog; 6 bandicoot; 7 buffalo; 8 dromedary; 9 caribou; 10 chipmunk; 11 dormouse; 12 earthworm; 13 squirrel; 14 giraffe; 15 glow-worm; 16 grasshopper; 17 hammerhead; 18 bumblebee; 19 jellyfish; 20 leopard.

Make a Bird (page 45)
Harrier

A Doggy Puzzle (page 46)
Greyhound; alsatian; retriever; beagle; poodle; setter; dachshund; spaniel; terrier; collie.

They're All Red (page 47)
1 Red admiral; 2 red deer; 3 red squirrel; 4 red spider; 5 redwing; 6 red grouse; 7 redworm.

In the Country (page 48)
Cow; horse; hare; pig; calf; lamb; chicken; goat; duck; goose; rat; mouse; rabbit.

It's the Size that Matters (page 49)
1 Giant clam; 2 large blue; 3 little plover; 4 bighorn; 5 great crested grebe; 6 small (or large) white.

Hidden Animals (page 50)
Mink; gopher; donkey; bandicoot; camel; llama; gnu; porcupine; tapir; ass; rabbit; giraffe; marmoset; tiger.

Beaks and Birds (page 51)

1 (Puffin) needs the beak on 4; 2 (ostrich) needs the beak on 6; 3 (owl) needs the beak on 9; 4 (flamingo) needs the beak on 7; 5 (spoonbill) needs the beak on 3; 6 (toucan) needs the beak on 8; 7 (sparrow) needs the beak on 1; 8 (hornbill) needs the beak on 2; 9 (pelican) needs the beak on 5.

Add an Animal (page 52)

1 Tortoiseshell; 2 scat; 3 skipper; 4 lemur; 5 panther; 6 bass; 7 dragonfly.

Change the X (page 53)

1 Rhinoceros; 2 dormouse; 3 dromedary; 4 elephant; 5 dragonfly; 6 gorilla; 7 hippopotamus; 8 humming bird; 9 kangaroo; 10 marmoset; 11 millipede; 12 octopus; 13 orang-utan; 14 partridge; 15 tortoise; 16 porcupine; 17 porpoise; 18 scorpion; 19 woodpecker; 20 alligator.

A Cat Comes First (page 54)

1 Catkin; 2 catmint; 3 catsear; 4 catstail; 5 catfish; 6 catbird.

Hidden Flowers (page 55)

1 Pansy; 2 daisy; 3 pink; 4 orchid; 5 anemone; 6 snowdrop; 7 aster; 8 rose; 9 dandelion; 10 peony.

All That Glitters (page 56)

1 Goldcrest; 2 goldeneye; 3 golden rod; 4 goldfinch; 5 goldfish; 6 Goldilocks; 7 golden eagle; 8 golden hamster; 9 golden mole; 10 golden pheasant.

An Animal Saying (page 58)

Don't put the cart before the horse.

Where do they Live? (page 59)
1 Blackbird - nest; 2 bee - hive; 3 otter - holt; 4 fox - earth;
5 squirrel - drey; 6 badger - sett; 7 hare - form; 8 pig - sty;
9 rabbit - warren; 10 horse - stable.

Bears About (page 60)
Polar; grizzly; kodiak; sun; black; brown.

Beautiful Butterflies (page 61)
1 Comma; 2 red admiral; 3 small brown or small white; 4 small
tortoiseshell; 5 brimstone.

Strange Animals (page 62)
1 (Zebra) needs the coat on 2; 2 (giraffe) needs the coat on 5;
3 (leopard) needs the coat on 1; 4 (panda) needs the coat on
3; 5 (lion) needs the coat on 6; 6 (fallow deer) needs the coat
on 4.

Hidden Insects (page 64)
1 Aphid; 2 mite; 3 bee; 4 beetle; 5 earwig; 6 flea; 7 lace wing;
8 louse; 9 wasp; 10 moth.

Coded Birds (page 65)
1 Thrush; 2 sparrow; 3 osprey; 4 swallow; 5 bluetit; 6 yellow
hammer; 7 partridge; 8 robin; 9 crow; 10 redwing.

Groups of Animals (page 66)
1 Gaggle; 2 flock; 3 drove; 4 pride; 5 sleuth; 6 down; 7 litter;
8 stud; 9 swarm; 10 flight; 11 pack; 12 herd; 13 school; 14 cete;
15 nest.

Mountain Animals (page 67)
Bear; wolf; leopard; ibex; yak; jackal.

Tree Quiz (page 68)
1 Horsechestnut; 2 mountain ash; 3 hazel; 4 willow (the cricket bat willow is grown for its wood); 5 yew; 6 oak; 7 plane; 8 elm; 9 ash; 10 Scots pine; 11 larch; 12 hawthorn; 13 dog (or wild) rose; 14 maple; 15 silver birch; 16 beech; 17 cedar of Lebanon; 18 holly; 19 because of its drooping branches; 20 alder.

Animal Crossword (page 70)
Across: 1 Gorilla; 4 antelope; 8 goat; 9 walrus; 12 fox; 13 ape; 15 stag; 16 stoat; 17 beaver; 20 deer; 24 hare; 26 lion; 27 rut; 28 tit; 30 hive; 33 frog; 34 pug; 35 wasps; 37 ass; 40 anvil; 42 bat; 43 teal; 44 gnat.

Down: 2 Ox; 3 llama; 5 newt; 6 loris; 7 cod; 10 snake; 11 mole; 14 panda; 16 seal; 18 vole; 19 rabbit; 21 eel; 22 gannet; 23 mare; 25 run; 28 thrush; 29 earwig; 30 horse; 31 slug; 32 avocet; 36 sloth; 38 knot; 39 jay; 41 leg.

Wild Flowers (page 72)
1 Buttercup; 2 water lily; 3 poppy; 4 sweet violet; 5 bluebell; 6 primrose; 7 bramble; 8 dog rose; 9 honeysuckle; 10 daisy.

Bird Sayings (page 73)
1 Lark; 2 bird; 3 crow; 4 chickens; 5 goose/gander; 6 owl; 7 bird; 8 feather; 9 coot; 10 eggs.

Animals Overseas (page 74)
1 Ostrich; 40 mph/64 kph; 2 Australia; 3 apes; 4 aardvark; 5 polar bear; 6 wolf; 7 river horse; 8 from its call; 9 caribou; 10 chamois; 11 opposum; 12 okapi; 13 orang-utan; Borneo and Sumatra; 14 kookaburra; 15 Colorado beetle; 16 hair; 17 largest flying bird; 18 koala, it feeds mainly on the leaves of the gum tree; 19 Haiti and Cuba; 20 bongo.

A Fishy Problem (page 77)

Bass; tench; minnow; cod; pike; sole; dace; bullhead; bream; carp; hake.
New fish: stickleback.

Discover the Deer (page 78)

Axia; red; fallow; moose; muntjac; sika; père david's.

Animal Word Square (page 79)

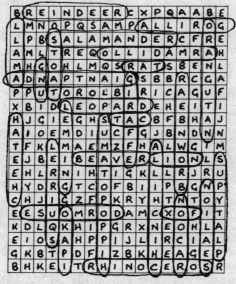

Leaves, Fruits and Seeds (page 80)

A (horse chestnut) goes with 4; B (scots pine) goes with 5; C (holly) goes with 1; D (alder) goes with 3; E (hazel) goes with 2; F (sycamore) goes with 8; G (beech) goes with 7; H (oak) goes with 6.

Weather Permitting (page 81)
1 Windscorpion; 2 thunderfly; 3 snow leopard; 4 clouded yellow; 5 rainbird; 6 rainbow trout; 7 lightning beetle; 8 storm petrel; 9 sun bear; 10 blow fly.

Take the Letters (page 82)
1 Ass; 2 blackbird; 3 finch; 4 panther; 5 whale; 6 mandarin; 7 mistletoe; 8 swordfish; 9 sloth; 10 rabbits; 11 wombat; 12 martin; 13 bats; 14 hen; 15 bushbaby.
Proverb: A bird in the hand is worth two in the bush.

Missing Vowels (page 85)
1 Elephant; 2 shearwater; 3 beaver; 4 kangaroo; 5 pintail; 6 dormouse; 7 rhinoceros; 8 salamander; 9 chameleon; 10 hartebeest.

More Birds (page 86)
1 Starling; 2 moorhen; 3 redstart; 4 wigeon; 5 pipit; 6 bullfinch; 7 greylag.

Animal Riddle (page 88)
Armadillo.

Hidden Birds (page 89)
1 Swan; 2 starling; 3 heron; 4 kite; 5 knot; 6 dove; 7 teal; 8 wren; 9 rook; 10 thrush.

Place Names (page 90)
1 Brent goose, 2 Camberwell beauty; 3 Colorado beetle; 4 Herb Paris; 5 London pride; 6 Canada goose; 7 African elephant; 8 Manx cat; 9 Galapagos tortoise; 10 Bengal tiger; 11 Arctic tern; 12 Portuguese Man-o-War; 13 Scots pine; 14 Norway spruce.

Come Fly with Us (page 92)
1 Damselfly; 2 dragonfly; 3 alderfly; 4 cranefly; 5 housefly; 6 butterfly; 7 sawfly; 8 mayfly; 9 horsefly.

Animal Riddle (page 93)
Hedgehog

The Name's the Same (page 94)
1 Swallow; 2 swift; 3 bunting; 4 skylark; 5 warbler; 6 cuckoo; 7 nightingale; 8 merlin; 9 wren; 10 hobby; 11 rail; 12 drill; 13 skate; 14 cricket; 15 grouse; 16 hog; 17 mule; 18 shrimp; 19 badger; 20 bat.

Hidden Fruit (page 96)
1 Melon; 2 olive; 3 banana; 4 fig; 5 apple; 6 peach; 7 lemon; 8 orange; 9 grape; 10 plum.

In the Country (page 97)
Hedge sparrow; pond skater; fieldfare; buttercup; cowslip; horsechestnut; foxglove; milkweed; tree creeper; gatekeeper.

From Beginning to End (page 98)
1 Tulip; 2 buttercup; 3 eagle; 4 mouse; 5 otter; 6 shrew; 7 daffodil; 8 badger; 9 rabbit; 10 squirrel; 11 hedgehog; 12 shrimp; 13 parrot; 14 viper; 15 elephant; 16 swallow; 17 osprey; 18 salmon; 19 redwing; 20 goats.

On the Seashore (page 100)
Crab; cockle; mussel; seaweed; herring gull; sea holly; shrimp.

Another Name for It (page 101)
1 Sponge; 2 mole; 3 ruff; 4 kite; 5 perch; 6 bass; 7 sole; 8 ray.

Whiter than White (page 102)
1 White admiral; 2 white bait; 3 white beam; 4 white front; 5 white fly; 6 white throat; 7 white worm; 8 white ant; 9 white fish; 10 white nettle.

Hook, Line and Sinker (page 103)
1 Stickleback; 2 plaice; 3 haddock; 4 pike; 5 salmon; 6 perch; 7 turbot; 8 eel.

Two Timing (page 104)
1 Buffalo and osprey; 2 swallowtail and bittern; 3 dragonfly and grass snake; 4 otter and salmon; 5 coltsfoot and fieldfare; 6 jackal and vulture; 7 elephant and whale; 8 buttercup and horse chestnut; 9 crocus and snowdrop; 10 kangaroo and koala.

Occupations (page 106)
Shepherd's purse; red admiral; butcher bird; soldier ant; cardinal beetle; engraver beetle; by-the-wind sailor; reeve's pheasant; archer fish; angler fish.

Hidden Birds (page 107)
Mistle thrush; redwing; sparrow; redshank; plover; starling.

Animal Sayings (page 108)
1 Take the bull by the horns; 2 never look a gift horse in the mouth; 3 don't put the cart before the horse; 4 a cat can look at a queen; 5 as mad as a March hare.

And so to the End (page 115)
1 Zorille; 2 zebra; 3 yucca; 4 yellowhammer; 5 zinnia; 6 yak.